# better together*

**\*This book is best read together, grownup and kid.**

**akidsbookabout.com**

a kids book about

™

# a kids book about<sup>™</sup>

GRATITUDE

by Ben Kenyon

# a kids book about™

Text and design copyright © 2019 by Ben Kenyon

Library of Congress Cataloging-in-Publication Data is available.

This book represents my personal experience and thus is not intended to be representative of every form or example of gratitude..

A Kids Book About Gratitude is exclusively available online on the a kids book about website.

To share your stories, ask questions, or inquire about bulk purchases (schools, libraries, and nonprofits), please use the following email address:

hello@akidsbookabout.com

www.akidsbookabout.com

ISBN: 978-1-951253-22-6

Printed in the USA

Peggy Drinkard, My Ma
Thank you for always leading by example.

# Intro

Take two seconds and think about a basic need that is automatic, breathing.

Do you stop and think about breathing or do you just wake up and breathe? Do you have to work in order to breathe? Do you put any effort into breathing or is it just natural?

Let's practice breathing. Inhale through the nose and exhale through the nose. Inhale through the nose and exhale through the mouth. How awesome is that?

This is so small and simple, yet this is one thing that gives you life. You walk because you're breathing, you talk because you're breathing and smile, you guessed it, because you're breathing.

Aren't you grateful for breathing?

Gratitude is the appreciation of the small moments that make the biggest impact in our lives.

HI, MY NAME IS BEN.

WHEN PEOPLE DESCRIBE
ME, THEY SAY I'M...

BOLD
AUTHENTIC

# INFLUENTIAL HYPE

(HYPE MEANS EXCITED ALL THE TIME)

BUT FEW KNOW
MY TRUE IDENTITY...

LET ME TELL YOU
A STORY...

WHEN I WAS LIVING
IN FLORIDA...

ONE DAY I WAS DRIVING
HOME FROM WORK...

AND I RAN OUT OF GAS.

BUMMER,

RIGHT?!

WELL, I HAD TO PUSH MY
CAR TO A GAS STATION.

BUT I REALIZED WHEN I
TRIED TO BUY GAS...

I DIDN'T HAVE ANY MONEY.

AND ON *TOP* OF THAT...

MY FATHER JUST
PASSED AWAY.

TO PUT IT SIMPLY...

I WASN'T HAVING A
GREAT DAY.

HOW WOULD YOU FEEL IF
THAT HAPPENED TO YOU?

IF YOUR DAY JUST SEEMED
TO KEEP GETTING WORSE?

HOW DO YOU THINK I FELT?

AT FIRST, PRETTY SAD.

THEN, CALM.

THEN...

I THOUGHT ABOUT
EVERYTHING I HAD...

AND THAT MADE ME
FEEL GREAT!

YOU SEE...

I HAVE A SECRET
TO TELL YOU...

I HAVE A...

SUPER

MY SECRET
SUPERPOWER CAN...

TURN BAD DAYS INTO GREAT ONES.

MAKE SAD SITUATIONS AWESOME.

BRING JOY WHEN THINGS GET HARD.

AND ALLOW ME TO APPRECIATE LIFE EVERY DAY.

MY SUPERPOWER IS CALLED

IT'S BETTER THAN FLYING
OR SUPER STRENGTH,
TRUST ME.

IT MEANS I CAN GIVE,
RECEIVE, AND APPRECIATE
KINDNESS ALL THE TIME.

IT'S SOMETHING I...

CHOOSE EVERYDAY.

BUILD STRONGER EVERYDAY.

AND FEEL EVERYDAY.

GUESS WHAT?!

YOU CAN HAVE IT TOO...

IF YOU WANT.

LET ME SHOW YOU HOW...

# FIRST

DISCOVER WHAT'S
ALREADY THERE.

YOUR LIFE IS PROBABLY
FULL OF ORDINARY,
BUT AMAZING
THINGS...

FOOD, FAMILY, CLOTHES, SUNSHINE, FRIENDS, PETS, AND TOYS.

RECOGNIZE THEM FOR WHAT THEY ARE, EVEN THOUGH THEY'RE ALWAYS THERE.

NEXT

LOOK PAST
DISTRACTIONS.

LIFE CAN BE FULL OF
SADNESS AND PAIN.

TO USE YOUR SUPERPOWER, YOU HAVE TO BE ABLE TO NOT JUST FOCUS ON THOSE THINGS.

BUT, LOOK PAST THEM.

# THEN

APPRECIATE ALL
YOUR GIFTS.

EACH AND EVERY
PLATE OF FOOD,

THE LAUGH YOU SHARE
WITH A FRIEND,

AND THE SHIRT YOU
WEAR TO SCHOOL...

IS SOMETHING YOU CAN
BE GRATEFUL FOR.

AND OFTEN WAS SOMETHING
GIVEN TO YOU.

BECAUSE, EVERYTHING
IS BETTER WHEN IT'S
A GIFT, ISN'T IT?

# LAST

EXPRESS
GRATITUDE.

GRATITUDE IS AT
ITS BEST, WHEN YOU
EXPRESS IT TO OTHERS
IN THE FORM OF...

GIVING, RECEIVING, THANKING, KINDNESS, AND SMILING.

GRATITUDE IS MEANT TO BE SHARED.

BUT EVERYONE KNOWS, EVERY SUPERPOWER HAS A FLAW...

SOME IMPOSSIBLE CRUSHING WEAKNESS...

JUST LIKE SUPERMAN'S WEAKNESS IS KRYPTONITE, GRATITUDE'S FLAW IS...

# DISTRA

CTION!

THE LESS YOU'RE ABLE TO SEE THE WONDERFUL AND ORDINARY GIFTS...

THE LESS YOU CAN BE GRATEFUL...

DISTRACTION MAKES A BIG DEAL OF THE BAD THINGS IN YOUR LIFE...

AND MAKES EVERYTHING ELSE DISAPPEAR.

BUT GRATITUDE HAS A SPECIAL WEAPON AGAINST DISTRACTION.

VISION!

FOR REALS!

GRATITUDE CAN SEE
THROUGH DISTRACTION,
TO ALL THOSE ORDINARY
GIFTS IN YOUR LIFE.

ALL THOSE GOOD THINGS
THAT ARE ALWAYS AROUND,
BUT YOU SOMETIMES
FORGET ARE THERE.

*GRATITUDE* IS MY SUPERPOWER...

AND IT CAN BE YOUR SUPERPOWER, TOO!

IF YOU CHOOSE IT.

SO CHOOSE
GRATITUDE TODAY!

AND WITH
PRACTICE AND
TIME, YOU'LL GROW
MORE POWERFUL EACH
AND EVERY DAY.

# Outro

**L**et's gooo!!! You and your kiddo are SUPER HEROES!!! WE OUT HERE!!! COME ON NOW!!!

Gratitude is the one superpower that not only makes your life better, but also impacts every person around you.

So how can you activate your kiddo every day to use their new superpower?

Tell them about what you're grateful for. Remind them that even though something might be good, they might not feel grateful for it automatically.

Then, have them write down or tell you one thing they are grateful for every day. This will help build their gratitude "muscles" so they become big and strong.

Help them look past distractions and appreciate all their gifts, both big and small, daily.

# find more kids books about

racism, feminism, creativity
money, depression, failure,
belonging, adventure,
cancer, body image,
and anxiety.

**akidsbookabout.com**

# share
# your read*

*Tell somebody, post a photo,
or give this book away to
share what you care about.